Weather

Weather

Selected Poems
1975-2005

Vyvyan Rothfeld-Brunst

Lilibug Publishing

Copyright © 2008 Vyvyan Rothfeld-Brunst.
ISBN 978-0-578-05512-1

All rights reserved. The use of any part of this publication, reproduced, transmitted in any form or by any means, electronic, mechanical, photocopying, recording, or otherwise, or stored in a retrieval system, without written consent of the publisher is an infringement of the copyright law.

Lilibug Publishing
5620 Fossil Creek Pkwy #12207
Fort Collins, CO 80525 USA

Front cover: painting by Jane A. Rothfeld.

Edited and typeset by the author. The poems are set in 12-point OpenType Century Schoolbook with 16 points of leading.

Printed & bound by Lulu.com.

"Declamatore" was previously published in *Arc 37* (Autumn 1996); "It's Just Like Showers," "Marriage Bed," "Summer Wedding," "One Hundred Names for Rain," "Early Spring," "Red Setter," "The Kids at Sir Sanford Fleming," "Bus Conversation," "June Evening," "Killing a Rabbit in the Painted Desert," and "Singing Inside" appeared in *The Ring in the Wood*; "Black Horse in a Washington Field," "Crow," "Drones," "Sibyl," "The Bee's Nest," "Teatime," "Winter Scene," and "Jigsaw" appeared in *Common Tongues*. "After Class" appeared under the title "All That (and the sidewalk tin)" and "Cannon Beach" appeared under the title "My Biography" in *Common Tongues*.

To Patrick Lane
kind enough to sign
Too Spare, Too Fierce

Other Books by Vyvyan Rothfeld-Brunst

Common Tongues (1980)
Natasha in the Pumpkin Patch (1987)
The Ring in the Wood (1996)

Table of Contents

Teatime/ 15
Black Horse in a Washington Field/ 16
Cassie/ 17
Cannon Beach/ 18
Crow/ 19
After Class/ 20

The Bee's Nest/ 25
Drones/ 28
Sibyl/ 29
Boy with a Gun/ 30
Winter Scene/ 31
Jigsaw/ 32
Summer Wedding/ 33
Marriage Bed/ 35
Nakina/ 37
Early Spring/ 39
Bus Conversation/ 40
Killing a Rabbit in the Painted Desert/ 41
Singing Inside/ 43

Haircut/ 45
One Hundred Names for Rain/ 46
Christmas Sonnet/ 48
Third Sonnet/ 49
English Lessons/ 50
Kite/ 51
Red Setter/ 53
The Kids at Sir Sandford Fleming/ 54
It's just like showers/ 57
Declamatore/ 58
June Evening/ 60

Safflower, I Love You/ 65
The Bear in the Buckwheat/ 66
Burrow Poem/ 68
Bigtooth Maple: 3 tankas/ 69
Graduation Day: 2 tankas/ 70
Ravine/ 71
Father Dying/ 74
The Penitent Brothers/ 76

Portland

Teatime

Your strange confusion
veils thin as tea bag veil
some potent determination
contained within and strained
against the teacup edge
it stains what once
was colourless and pure and heated.

Hardly offered but rejected.

Black Horse in a Washington Field at Six in the Evening from a Greyhound Bus

If it opened an eye the land would throb.
The fenceline runs a course to left and right,
a speculation in the mist.
The grass that feathers the hoof from a root
is everywhere, and indistinct.

In Geneva there was weathered
and just as still as this
a statue with its eyes as blank.

But you're not thinking of a past or time to come.
Just a field and a moment staring,
A steady rain like stone.

The bus window is kinder:
paints you lambent, black.
An exclamation in a field
that means nothing to you
and owes you nothing.

Cassie

Cassie honey
summers linger
on your memory
like a finger
hung on trinkets,
on ginger branches,
hardly hidden
in a thousand trances
I spent sleep-like,
sea-like, Cassie.

Hoping this'll reach you
as it leaves me.

Cannon Beach

When they come to write my biography
tell them that the desk inside my room
faces two great windows, many-paned
like an insect's eyes;
tell them that through the eyes
the hills of western Oregon
and the treetops rise,
the road to Cannon Beach
and the drift of seaweed
in the pre-dawn mist
before the fall of human feet
where countless broken bones
lie bleached and wetted every tide.

And that confronts the writer
seated like a convict
waiting for the verdict
carried on the air
between the mouth of western Oregon
and the prisoner.

Crow

He lets it be known
that he lends the tree
new grandeur.

Branch on branch,
the cloud mounts the thick stem:
an envelope of air.

They are older,
more ancient than want,
Cloud and Crow.

They grow around the tree
twin brothers
condescending to one another.

After Class

I hear the trains at night:
they couple in the yard.
Supermen clock in
and heavy axles push in grease,
polite for metal,
the black grease dragged
in the tie-built rumble
of the heavy freeway,
heading home.

This head collected pollen
on the homeward walk
from blue stalk shadows.
One o'clock, I moved
reluctant, parallel to the railyard
and the midtown smell.

Across the Willamette, across Ross Island
river winds brought screams of children
with a comic book taste of half past ten.

(Begin again.
Come right back in
and begin again,
holding the books
not quite so tight against the thigh
and the Pelican pen.)

And the turn and the fence
and the lights
that turn to yellow,
first to yellow, then to white.

Vancouver

The Bee's Nest

It was cool sometimes,
creeping in the pine and eucalyptus,
stealing through hidden spaces
where the season paled,
where summer staked a place
on every beach towel bleached.

I remember following her foot
on leafy earth like coffee grounds
still damp,
unctuous arms stitched tight,
tasting sweat on our noses
and our tongues
and sun and devils in our faces.

Alison was California
like the copses, a pulse wrung
from veins that pushed up trees
and pushed out beaches
into lethargic space:
the empty maternal air.

I remember winding
past the Spanish tower
in the air of blown geraniums
always dying.

I remember her smile:
a winking eyelit invitation.

California was Alison
in its least expression.

Thursday —
we counted
six or seven spider webs today.
I wonder if they trouble us
for being fine, a world
more secret than our own.
If that was why we knelt
in the long grass
and blew them out like sails.

If that was why
she placed her fingers
through the dew-jewelled loops
and swirled them to chaos.

The bee's nest was a stump —
an old oak
rotted, sealed,
and smelling of resin.
Friday morning off from school
we heaped mud and leaves
to stop the heart-shaped hole.

I remember Alison with a stick
and the rich swarm
that burst from the wood like fluid,
while she cried and cried
and ran with her insect headdress
pushing me away and crying
"Help me!"

I put out my hand to help
but she was too
concerned with punishment.

Drones

She lies smug as a queen bee
in the summer heat;
the hot wash of sprinklers.
Green, the pulse of thick earth
under her greenery.

I put on my black cap.
We administer to her smallest need
to the drone of grass machines
on her fat idleness.

Sibyl

Madame Elizabeth
deft as she is with cards
however compelling her eyes
muted with a gauze film,
her voice shuffling over my left shoulder
where she directs her prophesies
in a monotone.
She is no threat to you
dishing the Hanged Man
sincere as she is
with her faded print dress
and pudgy fingers
fingering the card.

She is no threat to you,
however menial you feel
beside her serving the coffee.
You have cast tomorrow
with a glance, and taken
all our future with a smile.

Boy with a Gun

We shared the sidewalk
and he, too old for lemonade,
his head so resolute it shook,
his fingers wrapped
around the plastic gun,
his voice too guttural
for ten years old,
shouted "Pow!"
and the arm recoiled
as I walked on past his house.

I wanted to say:
that isn't the way it is at all.
You hear the footsteps first,
the voice is soft:
"Stop or you're dead."
The gun seems far too small,
winking in the streetlight.
The ring comes off too slowly
and the boy is nervous
when he whispers
keep walking.

Winter Scene

Does this mean anything to you?

Through the night
the forest was iced
and you are not a woman
but a bird, bobbing
on the snowed branch,
pioneering the rebirth
of the forest
with a sweet assessment
of your territory.

Jigsaw

Treat this poem like a jagged piece.
Like all the others
treat it gently.
Roll it if you like
along the lips
or mind or fingertips.
Don't mutilate, leave   it
bell-like, round and numb don't bend
the meaning or the edge or force it
dumb and helpless where it will not go.
It's made from pain and patience, glaze
and coloured, sky and earth you recognize
and something that will not make sense
right now. It will. In time. Fit it with
the others. They'll only give a view
of what I might have been
                                      and am.

Summer Wedding

New married, they lived one summer
by an apple tree,
and watched the fruit
turn green, then oxblood red.
And watched the sun
and watched the shingled sea.

August came, untended
in the long grass.
At picking time
he found a bright pot
and shook the apples down,
his hands around the branches.

He was awkward in his wedding ring
(his smallest finger rubbed it,
like a tongue with a new tooth):
the ring, smooth as bone against the trunk,
and the thick branch like
a stevedore's arm.

Where apples fell
they stewed in pockets
of unclipped grass,
in earthen cider smells,
in a garden quick with snakes
and sowbugs.

He stood among them
in a fine independence,
satisfied to not be
mad with growing,
while Sara watched him
from the kitchen.

She must have seen him as he was:
simple and apart,
and not some mythic thing —
legs, wrapped
and rooted to the earth by snakes,
his arms in apples,
and all his skyward fingers, leaves.

Marriage Bed

When she was young
she would sing in her ptarmigan throat
a sound like flutes.

We were green flesh.
Our thoughts ran together like acids,
and she sang, when she was nineteen.

On a California rail,
her voice among the firs
and the fog, older than them.

I built her a wedding bed
from hemlock, spruce, and pine.
She sleeps among my whittled angels.

Unsinging she cries now.
In our wedding bed
her tears become diamonds

pressed by the moon
from her ancestral pain.
From some cavernous pain.

When I enter her
she oils the sheets,
resinous as myrrh.

She rests her eyes
from their inlaying
on my arm — her walnut eyes.

There is no wealth
that does not come
from the body of my lover.

Rising for work, with a handful of gems,
we sweep away
the amethysts of her bleeding.

Nakina

Three days out of Vancouver
at three in the morning
for stealing a pillow
they threw a drunk off the train
at Nakina.

The rest of us, discreet as chrysalids,
glued by our mouths to seat backs
arranged squares of sanitized foam
rented from the steward.

Doped with lemon drops,
crackling like a bad radio
the wrappers of Fox's Glacier Mints,
or tucking into sloe-eyed folds
a bag of sourdough rolls,
we ate continuously
the half-breadth of the continent.

And in the night
the big-faced drunk across the aisle
tossed suddenly when the attendant
tried to retrieve his pillow,
explaining that they must be paid for,
that she had already told him once before.
"Bitch!" he muttered
and shifted, ignoring her.

He cried when he saw RCMP
the yellow bands of their pant legs,
the cruiser, its red light wet
on the snow near the station at Nakina.
His mouth soured like a hand
curled in on itself, like a new fern.

What has he heard of Nakina?
Do the trees creak with petty thieves?
Does the museum mount snapshots
of blank-faced vigilantes
turned away from the swinging dead,
sober now, his mouth stuffed with pillow?

We woke with the crumbs of dreams
in shirtpockets, misting the glass
with our penitent breath:
You've got the wrong man, we said.
They took away the wrong man in Nakina.

Early Spring

The chestnuts on May Day
holding their great blossoms
like menorahs,
confused in the dark of the spring,
might have thought
it was safe.
But still counting "one thousand,
two thousand,
three thousand ..."
dressed in his white petticoat
stands the wolf.

Bus Conversation

Their voices, fatted
with gossip and
nimble as bats spun out of the dark
recall backshed bottles
weeping unpronounceable spirits.

And their scarves
touch singingly, the two
nodding Easter eggs
of their heads spring and relax,
their mouths red
with exclamations.

A ruddy hand
mottled like sausage
touches her sister's
as they pass the Ukrainian church
with its gilded saints.

A man gets up,
a good Canadian man
in a doeskin shirt, leans
cheek to jowl with this
good Canadian woman.
"Can't you speak English?" he says.

Killing a Rabbit in the Painted Desert

The humourless skies of Arizona
made this ground.
The city's wet bus windows slip away.
It is a world of bones; on mine
the skin slides like leather on the cow.
The two of us, skeletal in the cockpit
of our rented Ford, respire.

My knuckles change gears,
our eyes suck in the orange rock.
In some primitive part, knowing it
they know it.

We feel clean:
our sweat cleans us.

The rabbits that shoot from the sagebrush
make us laugh.
And then one leaps at the wheel
fired like a rocket in the dark.
I gauge its passing,
wishing it gone.
But the car hiccups,
swallows it
and passes on.

This morning, cutting a coupon
from the local paper
we walked into a rock shop
and bought a piece of petrified wood.
Rabbits and wood.
They do not seem to have learned with time.
There is no thought to them.

Surely, if that rabbit had thought
he would not have jumped; if that wood
had thought he would be living still.

And they would be driving,
they would be driving
through the Painted Desert.
The two of them.
The rabbit would be driving.
The petrified wood would
be in the passenger's seat.

They would hit us,
and tomorrow
the coyotes will come, and the ants,
and tomorrow there will be bones
like whistles for the grass.

Singing Inside

I couldn't be a priest.
Visions rarely come to them.
But every other girl in Guadeloupe
looks up to the suspirating meadow,
the lime tree itching against the sky,
the water breaking from the rock,
her mother's tears streaming in the clay
and from the hut on a feast day
the singing inside.

But I would be a black girl
on a Sunday morning, swinging
centrifugal on the lamppost
on San Pablo Avenue, while her momma says,
"Don't you dirty that dress!"
Grinning, her head a brown berry.
Across the street from the Dyno-Burger
the Baptist church; I stop to hear
the singing inside.

More easily, much more easily,
I could be a hunchback poet
wearing wool in summer, absently
rubbing the dust of pencils,
forgetting the cat's dinner,
wrapped in the dumb conspiracy of words

like a World War Two cryptographer
in a hole in London, trying to decode
the singing inside.

Or swimming in the darkness
of the river, muscled like a thought
that thinks of the sea
between the mill and the child's first
seaward step, singing the hope
of the sun-swimming salmon
returning to the eagle-hung
stream at Brackendale, red
with the singing inside.

Haircut

I cannot help thinking
that there is a connection
between the yellow leaf
you picked up on our walk
and said you wanted to print
in four colours (the last one red)
and for which you said only
a German word would do, suggesting
rückblick, rückenflosse, rückenflug —

and the pregnant Filipino woman
who cut my hair in the second week of October
with grim assurance,
like the butcher of an ancient hecatomb,
like a mole, like a lacerating birch.
The only one of them who finished the job
without a word
who nodded when she was done
as though this cut growth
was nothing new.

One Hundred Names for Rain

Someone told me the Inuit
have one hundred words for snow,
but I have not heard one of them.
And now they tell me,
like the story of the lemmings,
that may be wrong.

But in Vancouver
they have one hundred words
for rain.
Ignoring those unprintable
they still have twenty,
and leaving out those
understood only by the geese
in Stanley Park,
they still have twelve.

I have lent five of these to a friend
with a Canada Council grant
and I hoard the remaining seven.

The first is piss.
The second, fenemante.
The third — Lord Gingerbiscuit.
The fourth drifts in from the mill.
The fifth, on a gillnetter.

The sixth is the sudden rain
that knocks down the cherry blossoms.
The seventh lies
in the mountains whispering
what it knows of you.

Christmas Sonnet

The grand fir that we ferried home and stood
incongruous and plain — though branches bent
soon filled this synthesis of brass and wood
and polyester curtain with its scent.

But nothing decked it out nor beautified
it yet; displaced but perfect on its stem
it swayed to songs from schoolboys rarefied
as full-cheeked choristers and bowed to them.

And while it dies a little every day
and every day a few more needles drop,
we grow more polished putting bells and clay-
cast figurines upon its bristling top.

Keep lessons in your books, but I would try
to learn to live by learning how to die.

Third Sonnet

At Christmas time it snowed, and when it snowed
the flakes were driven into fits of frost
that gathered on the cherry boughs and bowed
these branches; under their white weight lay lost

some mechanism of triumphal spring:
the thought of greener buds, the genius
return of daffodils that Aprils bring.
And so, the snow lay green and marvellous.

It rained in February like a weir
of clouds had burst up on the coastal range
and emptied on the cherries every tear.
And so the rain fell withering and strange.

Do cherries love the grey skies and the blue
as much as I love all the moods of you?

English Lessons

The pebble of a word
drops through the
smooth circumference
of my student's ear.
It falls unbending
with a kind of murder in its flight
(the ruthlessness of bulls
and plumb bobs, and pigeon shot).
Between his pauses
I listen for its splash
so far below the ligature of speech
one thinks one doesn't hear.

Minds are like wells, I suppose —
or polished steel that bounces
words like light
from the cowling of an F-16.
I have seen sixth-grade girls
incinerate a thought, sucking up the ash;
at other times, ambivilent:
a flower receiving a fly.
Nothing worries like a word.
What have I done?
And why this word? Why then?
And what creeps up
from that well:
The cannibal bird,
the crooked beak of heaven?

Kite

When first it had flown
he felt foolish to have lain in bed, edgy,
doubting the wind at Vanier Park
was strong enough for kites.
But Roger said, "You wait. It'll go."
They'd seen the sky fill up with row on row:
diamond and delta, box kites,
winged box, and even Indian fighting kites,
shocking the clouds like blossoms
on a pale tweed suit.

His was no beauty, just dowel and glue
and butcher paper, but it flew on the third pass
when his brother turned toward the bay
and ran a little north, northwest.

Then taking back the spindle once again
he eased the cord uncertainly, in starts,
feeling at eight what it means to keep and hold
a thing that wants to pull away
and wants to stay — like fish and clumsy kisses do.

For almost half an hour he was happy
to play captain to the swinging string
watching the kite become a stamp,
a thumbprint in the gray and then
imperceptible: a narrow smoke,

a speck he realized was a bird
drifting above the tension in his hands.

Well before he was sure the string went slack.
Bowing and never going taut, though
the brothers squinted for ages into the accepting air.
They found it in an oak,
full sixty feet above the parking lot,
too high for pulling down.

"We'll make another." And so they left.
And it seemed to the kite, tethered in his oak,
that for the first time they were leaving:
the flight before was a childhood they had shared,
agreeing to lose themselves a while, and then
in silent counting reel each other in.
But the boy with the strong hands
turned and walked away and crossed the street
until at last, far into the bright day
he disappeared from view.

Red Setter

A man with a red setter
passed us in
Pacific Spirit Park.

A cedar stump crumbles:
mineral pigments
richer than coho flesh.

For a moment
everything became wood:
our footfalls soft with it,

the setter's carmine coat,
the grunt of the man
on the trail

his lashes
finer
than fiddleheads.

The Kids at Sir Sandford Fleming

They build nylon sandcastles
at the base of the hoops —
casual things.
It is their heraldry:
the jackets with
stripes, swooshes, slashes;
the dismembered bull,
the rage-wrinkled panther.
Every hook, bill, and claw
in the wild
cast off for a moment
in bright piles at the end of the key.

The boys themselves
loose-limbed, solemn,
transfigure chivalry.

They have stripped themselves
of armour, and only their shoes advertise.
Bird-thin and barely breathing
they stutter
their steps, playing possum
hiding the ball, saying

"Y'see ... I can do that."
They play the African game,
the game played on the Serengeti
between the zebra and the cheetah,
the game played by the Punjabi kids
on Forty-ninth and Main.

But these boys,
black-haired, solemn,
are Cantonese.

They have stripped themselves
of language, and only their eyes
speak by looking where they are not going;
they shuffle their steps, syncopating,
slipping the ball
where they are not looking.
They dance the African dance,
where the pygmy dance the prey
where St. George dances the dragon
where Sir Sandford Fleming
(whoever he was)
dances the Canadian Shield.

Y'see, says the shooter,
hitting only net,
his wrist in midair like a heron's head.
Y'see, say the others
celebrating his shot
with their disinterest.
Y'see it's the same game.
Cool is colourless.

It's just like showers

The trees pour down viridian.
A man on a piebald mare knits
a path between the puddles,
smiling.
His goat's beard,
sharpened to a point,
could scrub pine tar off a briar.
"It's just like showers, ain't it," he says,
"to fall on sound fields."

Declamatore

Taking a stump for his lectern
he arranges a page turned out of his pocket.
A yellow ball,
a ball resembling clay,
which he rolls with a thick hand
into the flat of the cedar.

Once there were words.
The page was new, veined
with blue ink
like a suckling.
But the forest took them first.
It rained; a drizzle fell
from the lodgepole pine,
a fine mantilla fell
on his fingers
where they worried with paper
and the running ink.

Once there were whorls
milled in the paper,
ridges like those of his thumb.
Enjoying their feel, drily enjoying
he had left for the forest.
But the forest took them.

It rained; a syllable fell
from the sycamore,
a veil more gentle
than thinking
on his fingers where
they evened the smooth, pale page.
On that day he did not speak.

The ferns breathed out instead.
Mosses sweat into pools, chickadees
jibed and jigged
in the chokecherry bushes.

Two hundred mornings pass
in the same way.

Approaching the stump he removes
from his pocket an earthcoloured pea
soft as hashish
which he crumbles with thick fingers
into the flat of the cedar.
He presses the grains of his words
into the lichen and the old sawcut,
into the salt and the seeping damp,
and reads by heart
the ring in the wood.

June Evening

Before my wife left on a retreat
I took a picture of her
in a park with buttercups.

They were wild then,
bright as sulphur on the North Shore docks.
They seemed to eat her up.

In the photograph she is sitting
in a chrome green field
and the buttercups crowd on her shoulders.

Perhaps it is that way with colour:
if you put two together
sometimes they eat each other.

I have seen it before.
It was a picture of the Earth.
The stars were eating it.

Fort Collins

Safflower, I Love You
(on a railroad trestle outside Spokane)

Safflower, I love you.
I am waiting like these trestle timbers
for the weight
of the few seconds of your eyes.

No more mostly right and mostly wrong,
I'll fit between the precipice and pine.
I am fully paid, the forest's priest:
when I have married every leaf
to every restless blade of grass
I'll pick you softly like a young girl's sigh
and we'll ride forever
this carousel of cloud.

The Bear in the Buckwheat

In Cape Breton perhaps some fiddler knows:
it's the only place I've tracked the phrase,
a reel by that name that plays in the Dungreen Set
after "The Primrose Lasses".

And sure, it could be that for him
there was no connection.
When he came out with the line one morning
at a sales meeting, off-hand and slightly abashed,
like a good Canadian, it was:
"So I told him where
the bear shits in the buckwheat."

Now, when the rubber hits the road,
when the hens come home to roost, I'd heard,
but not this fertile idiom.

About bears I know little,
but I do know this:
it's always the imagined bear we fear the most;
the real bear roots in the furze,
registers the toe-tipping hiker,
and then turns away to his termites and his truth.

The image remains from that day —
the bear's brown flanks disappearing
through the bushes,
the stalks shuffling shut
behind his strength,
the rooks wheeling in the prairie sky,
and the field left undisturbed for memory.

For Jeff B., dead of a heart attack

Burrow Poem

They say the ermine will kill
even when it is not hungry,
slipping through fields
like a shade of dry corn,
a whisper of light from a passing car,
and then quick at the back of the neck.
Even mastiffs stay in the barn.
The ermine, they tell us,
takes the den of its prey,
jealous of the memory
of the poor beast's comfort.

At sixteen my words were clumsy things.
They have changed colour in the snow,
marked by cinders from railyard fires.
They have grown sharp rubbing themselves
against the leather strop of better writers.
So now I send them out in the dark.

When they don't come back
I imagine them warm
in the snowbanks of skulls
shuffling uneaten matter
to the mouth of the den.
The arctic night dressing itself in snow,
hiding the moon for camouflage.

Bigtooth Maple: 3 tankas

the bigtooth maple
at the end of the driveway
turns red as we watch
autumn begins its swelling
pregnant again: leaves don't lie

halloween pumpkin
the kids bring their scoops and knives
newspaper and pens
already holidays start
but this year I carve no mouth

they are getting old
the children cut no paper
paint no harvest scenes
but wet on the north window
a leaf blows against the glass

Graduation Day: 2 tankas

in the photograph
my father's seersucker suit
is too big for him
he will die four months after
this, my graduation day

north of the city
near the edge of a small lake
scarred with august fires
we drink ten year old champagne
the green shoots soft at our feet

Ravine

She thought it was late for winter
the sun bloodless in the south,
but they drove all the same
through the foothill farms
surprised at paint ponies and cattle
still in the fields, in the weeks-old snow.

There was a trail up the mountain
along a creek they'd taken
when the wild geranium bloomed
and sand lilies set themselves, discreet
as old money, in the prairie grass.
She hummed on the long drive
through the window, smoking.

At the mill house they sat in
the absent embroidery of sound:
chickens on the flagstone, dull percussion
of axes in the woodpile, and but
for the constant stream even now
in the ice everything ached
with leaving and being gone.

Not knowing if it would take them back
they followed the creek-side trail
each step doubting the last.
Until at the lightless bottom
where the ice had forgotten
what it kept
she stopped and waited for him.

The river bank unwound.
Rocks poked from the snow,
fat from hibernation.
Vines slipped from treetops
and the dead stream danced.
Mayflies in the rosiers
flew out of season.

She said our love, my love
survived longer than dew
when we were both about twelve
and sin was still new.
That was love, my love,
instead of the air
when we lay in the park
in the nest of my hair.
(The impressions we made
in the bank are still there.)

Our love, my love, was
all that I knew, it's all
that I know and know that I knew.

And then she tied up her boots
and swept up her hair.
And she hummed on the long drive back
through the window, smoking.

Father Dying

He used to tell stories of how
my mother would visit him at Oxford
and cook three-course meals on a single burner
while they sported the oak
which, he explained, meant
they kept the big wood door closed.

At the end he drank so much
telephone calls didn't reach him.
They fell through the wire
and you shied from his thick, warm voice.
His great chest shrank at seventy —
the clear-skinned youth
who scored three tries
the day I was born.

In the hospital, nurses fluttered
like sheets through the hallways.
It was a fine day
and they also were clouds.
I thought of that British summer,
the one all Englishmen remember
whether they were alive or not yet born
or dying in the air in Spitfires.

That was his — the tea on the grass,
and the big beneficent clouds
saying they would also be there
that day in Kelowna.

But he didn't speak.
I made some joke to his jaundiced head
about how I hadn't expected
to see him so soon
and took my place.
His breathing filled the room.

When it stopped his wife cried
and shouldered out, ignoring
my mothering arms.
I crept back in before they took his eyes.
Kissed his yellow brow,
our skin briefly the same.

The Penitent Brothers

The soap plant flowers in summer
but the leaves come early, sinuous
as Javanese daggers.
In the old west men lathered their hair
with the juice from the bulb,
healed poison oak, killed fish in the streams.

At the foot of the Turquoise Mountain
they are more devout.
By March the leaves of the plant
finger out in cat-o'-nine-tail clumps
and they clean away sin
on the backs of the Penitent Brothers.

(When they lashed Rafael to the cross
on Good Friday in a canyon out of town
he cried like a child for the nails:
Hay! Que estoy deshonrado!
His arms swelled purple and he groaned
in spite of the shame.)

While the village sleeps
the soap plant blooms in the hot afternoon,
its thin white petals curled back
like an ecstasy of saints,
stalks so delicate the flower seems
to float in the air, feeling for the sun.

www.ingramcontent.com/pod-product-compliance
Lightning Source LLC
Chambersburg PA
CBHW071743040426
42446CB00012B/2448